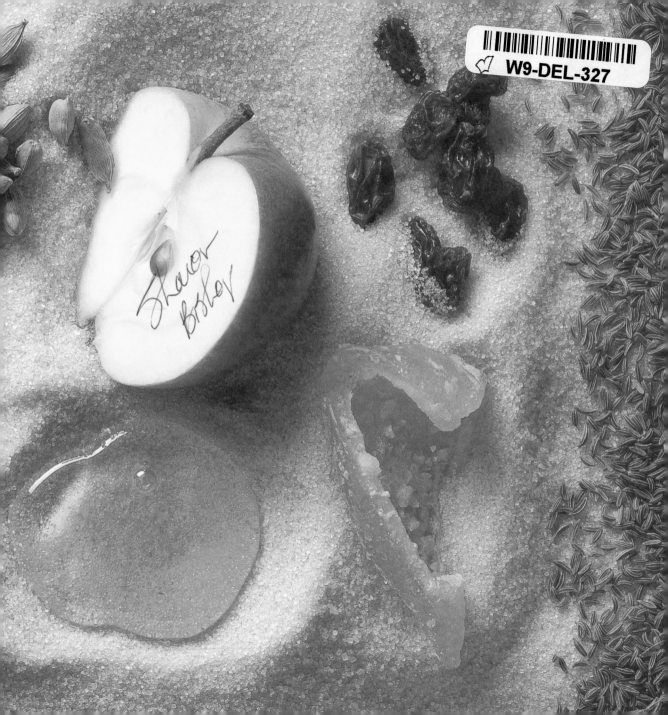

Sharon
Bishop

IRRESISTIBLE
COOKIES
&BISCOTTI

IRRESISTIBLE
COOKIES
& BISCOTTI

LINDA COLLISTER
Photography by
Patrice de Villiers

RYLAND
PETERS
& SMALL

London New York

Art Director **Jacqui Small**

Art Editor **Penny Stock**

Editor **Elsa Petersen-Schepelern**

Photography **Patrice de Villiers**

Food Stylist **Linda Collister**

Stylist **Penny Markham**

Production **Kate Mackillop**

To Daniel

Notes: Ovens should be preheated to the specified
temperature—if using a fan-assisted oven, adjust time and
temperature according to the manufacturer's instructions.

First published in the USA as *Basic Baking Cookies* in 1997
This edition published in 2000 by
Ryland Peters & Small, Inc.,
150 West 56th Street, Suite 6303, New York, N.Y. 10019

10 9 8 7 6 5 4 3 2 1

Text © Linda Collister 1997
Design and photographs © Ryland Peters & Small 1997

Printed and bound in China by Toppan Printing Co.

ISBN 1-84172-102-6

A CIP catalog record for this book is available from
the Library of Congress.

CONTENTS

homemade
cookies

A homemade cookie is a small luxury. It turns a coffee-break or a midnight snack into a moment of sheer pleasure—it's a little self-indulgence to warm your own day, or hospitality to brighten someone else's. Making cookies is easy enough, but a few pointers may be helpful. Most importantly, you need good ingredients for good results. I always use unrefined, **pure cane sugars** (except refined confectioners' sugar for decoration), because I find they have a slightly deeper flavor. Shown left, from top are raw sugar, superfine sugar, dark and light brown sugar, confectioners' sugar, and ordinary sugar. I prefer **sweet butter**: the taste is better and the cook, rather than the manufacturer, controls how much salt goes in the recipe.

I also prefer medium or large **eggs** and always use them at room temperature.

Organic and stoneground flours are now sold in most of the bigger supermarkets—I always use them because they are healthier and have better flavor, but ordinary flours can also be used in these recipes.

Nuts should be as fresh as possible: the oils they contain quickly turn rancid when exposed to air, so always store open packages in the freezer.

Use plain **chocolate** with at least 70 percent cocoa solids: supermarket own-labels are usually of very good quality and value. Some of the recipes in this book use white chocolate—use best-quality, and not children's white bars.

When using **lemon or orange zest**, use unwaxed fruit and wash the fruit well before removing the zest.

Best-quality **real vanilla extract** (the finest is from Mexico or Madagascar) should always be used. Because vanilla is expensive, some of the extract available is either low-grade or fake and chemical, and so smells and tastes very harsh. It is worth investing in good tools—they make baking easier and more successful.

Accurate scales and measuring spoons are essential. Teaspoons and tablespoons should all should be measured level unless the recipe calls for a rounded or heaped spoonful.

Electric food mixers and processors don't

just save time, they also make complicated recipes easier, less messy, and less exhausting. Cookies scorch easily, so thin, cheap **baking trays** can ruin the best recipe and the most careful preparation. Heavy, professional-quality trays or those specially made for cookies are wise investments and last a lifetime.

Airtight containers are vital for **storage**—cookies quickly lose their crispness, and often their shape, in humid conditions.

An **oven thermometer** is also very useful (many thermostats are unreliable). Each oven is an individual—most are temperamental. Learn how yours behaves, how quickly it warms up, how well it retains heat, and where the hot spots are. Baking times in these recipes cannot be more than guidelines, so know your oven, and watch your cookies carefully. Check the manufacturer's handbook if you are using a fan oven, or for guidance on shelf positions.

Two versions of a classic *cookie.*
oatmeal cookies

1 cup stoneground
whole-wheat flour

a good pinch of salt

1 teaspoon baking powder

⅔ cup rolled oats

1½ tablespoons sugar

¾ stick butter, chilled and diced

one 3-inch round cookie cutter

several baking trays, greased

Makes about 16

Put all the ingredients in a food processor and whizz until the dough comes together. (In very cold weather, you may have to work the lumps of dough together with your hands.)

Turn out the dough onto a lightly floured surface, and roll out to about ¼ inch thick. Using a 3-inch cookie cutter, cut the dough into rounds. Knead the trimmings together, re-roll, then cut out more rounds.

Arrange the cookies on the prepared trays and prick them well with a fork. Bake in a preheated oven at 375°F for about 12 to 15 minutes until they turn color slightly at the edges.

Remove from the oven and let cool on the baking trays for 3 to 4 minutes until firm enough to transfer to a wire rack. Let cool completely, then store in an airtight container. Eat within 1 week, or freeze for up to 1 month.

Variation:

Savory Oatmeal Cookies

Make the dough as in the main recipe, reducing the quantity of flour and adding the spices. Proceed as in the main recipe, and serve with cheese.

Reduce the sugar in the main
recipe to ¾ tablespoon
Add ¼ teaspoon curry powder or
garam masala*, or 1 teaspoon of
ground cinnamon or ginger

Makes about 16

*Available in Asian stores and
gourmet shops.*

oatmeal
raisin cookies

Mix the flour with the salt, baking powder, and oats.
Using a wooden spoon or electric mixer, cream the butter, sugar, and vanilla until fluffy.
Using your hands or a wooden spoon, gradually work in the flour mixture and dried fruit, then knead the mixture until it comes together. Roll it into balls about 1 inch across.
Place the balls well apart on the baking trays, then flatten them slightly with your fingers.
Cook in a preheated oven at 350°F for about 10 to 12 minutes or until golden.
Cool on the baking tray for a couple of minutes until firm enough to transfer to a wire rack.
Let cool completely, then store in an airtight container and

Make these cookies with dried sour cherries or dried cranberries instead of raisins—for an unusual and flavorful alternative.

1⅔ cups self-rising flour

a pinch of salt

1 teaspoon baking powder

2⅓ cups rolled oats

1 cup plus 2 tablespoons sweet butter, at room temperature

1 cup superfine
or granulated sugar

½ teaspoon real vanilla extract

⅓ cup raisins, dried sour cherries, or dried cranberries

several baking trays, greased

Makes about 32

13

old-fashioned gingersnaps

2⅓ cup self-rising flour

a pinch of salt

1 cup superfine or granulated sugar

1 tablespoon ground ginger

1 teaspoon baking soda

1 stick sweet butter

¼ cup golden syrup* or corn syrup

1 large egg, beaten

several baking trays, greased

Makes 30

*Available in larger supermarkets and gourmet shops.

Sift the flour into a mixing bowl with the salt, sugar, ginger, and baking soda. Heat the butter and syrup very gently in a small pan, mixing occasionally, until the butter melts. Let cool until just warm, then pour onto the dry ingredients. Add the egg and mix thoroughly.

Using your hands, roll the dough into 30 walnut-sized balls. Place the balls well apart on the prepared trays, then flatten slightly with your fingers.

Cook in a preheated oven at 325°F for about 15 to 20 minutes or until golden brown. Remove from the oven and leave on the trays for a minute to firm up, then transfer to a wire rack to cool completely.

Store in an airtight container and eat within 1 week, or freeze for up to 1 month.

If you like gingersnaps chewy, cook them for about 15 minutes until just firm—or if you prefer them crunchy, leave them in the oven for just a few minutes longer.

A *traditional* spicy cookie with sweet candied peel.

spice cookies

⅔ cup all-purpose flour

a pinch of salt

1 teaspoon baking powder

½ teaspoon baking soda

1 teaspoon ground ginger

½ teaspoon ground cinnamon

1½ tablespoons superfine or granulated sugar

2 tablespoons sweet butter, chilled and diced

1 tablespoon mixed peel, very finely chopped

3 tablespoons golden syrup* or corn syrup

several baking trays, greased

Makes about 20

*Available in larger supermarkets and gourmet shops.

Sift the flour into a mixing bowl with the salt, baking powder, baking soda, ginger, and cinnamon. (The combination of the two leavening agents is what makes these cookies crack.) Stir in the sugar. Add the cold chunks of butter and rub the mixture together with your fingertips until it resembles fine crumbs. Stir in the mixed peel, then the syrup, to make a firm dough. (In cold weather, warm the syrup after measuring, but before adding it to the mixture.)

Using your hands, roll the dough into about 20 marble-sized balls. Space them well apart on the prepared baking trays. Bake in a preheated oven at 400°F for about 7 minutes or until golden.

Remove from the oven and let cool on the trays for a couple of minutes. Transfer to a wire rack to cool completely.

Store in an airtight container and eat within 1 week, or freeze for up to 1 month.

Crisp, *light, icebox cookies—great on their own, or perfect with ice-creams and fruit salad.*

lemon poppyseed
cookies

1⅓ cups all-purpose flour

a pinch of salt

½ cup confectioners' sugar

¼ cup superfine
or granulated sugar

the grated zest of 1 lemon

2 teaspoons poppy seeds

1 stick sweet butter,
chilled and diced

1 egg, beaten

several baking trays,
lightly greased

Makes about 26

Put the flour, salt, sugars, grated lemon zest, and poppy seeds into a food processor and combine thoroughly. Add the cold chunks of butter and process until the mixture resembles fine crumbs. Add the egg and process again until the dough clumps together.

Shape the dough into a log about 3 inches in diameter and wrap it in foil. Chill until hard—at least 2 hours, or up to 1 week. The mixture can be sliced and baked when needed. When you are ready to bake the cookies, slice the logs into rounds about ¼ inch thick, and place them slightly apart on the prepared baking trays.

Bake in a preheated oven at 350°F until the edges are just beginning to turn golden brown—about 10 to 12 minutes. Transfer to a wire rack, and let cool.

Store in an airtight container and eat within 5 days, or freeze for up to 1 month.

ginger shortbread

1⅓ cups all-purpose flour

2 oz. fine oatflour

1 teaspoon ground ginger

½ teaspoon baking soda

½ cup plus 1 tablespoon
light brown sugar

1 piece preserved ginger in syrup,
drained and coarsely chopped

1 stick sweet butter,
chilled and diced

one 8-inch square pan,
well greased

Makes 9 squares

Mix all the ingredients except the butter in a food processor until they form the texture of coarse sand. Add the cold chunks of butter, then process until you have fine crumbs. Do not overwork the mixture—it should not form a dough.

Set aside 4 tablespoons of the crumbs. Tip the rest into the prepared pan and press them into an even layer with the back of a spoon. Sprinkle the reserved crumbs on top.

Using a round-bladed knife, score the shortbread into 9 squares. Bake in a preheated oven at 350°F for about 25 minutes or until they are just beginning to turn golden. Remove from the oven.

Cut along the scored lines, but leave the shortbread to cool in the pan before turning out.

Store in an airtight container and eat within 1 week, or freeze for up to 1 month.

*Three wonderful shortbreads—one with **ginger** flavor, another with green, unsalted pistachio nuts, and a third with a crunchy, **sugary** crust, named after Demerara, Guyana, which produces some of the world's best sugar.*

demerara shortbread

Using a wooden spoon or electric mixer, beat the butter until creamy, then beat in the caster sugar and vanilla extract, if using. Continue beating until the mixture is light and fluffy. Sift the flour with the rice flour and salt, then add to the mixing bowl. Work the dough with your hands until it comes together, then knead gently for a few seconds.

Form the dough into a log shape 6 x 3 inches. Roll in the raw or white sugar until evenly coated. Wrap in foil or greaseproof paper and chill until firm—about 20 minutes.

Unwrap the log and slice into ½-inch rounds. Arrange slightly apart on the prepared baking trays, prick with a fork, then chill for about 15 minutes until firm.

Bake in a preheated oven at 350°F for about 15 minutes until firm but not colored.

Cool for a couple of minutes, then transfer to a wire rack to cool completely. Store in an airtight container and eat within 1 week, or freeze for up to 1 month.

¾ cup sweet butter, at room temperature

½ cup superfine or granulated sugar

2–3 drops real vanilla extract (optional)

1⅔ cups all-purpose flour

⅓ cup rice flour, ground rice, or cornstarch

a pinch of salt

3–4 tablespoons raw or white sugar

one 3-inch round plain cutter

several baking trays, greased

Makes about 16

Variation:

Pistachio Shortbread

Make the dough as in the main recipe, adding the pistachios but omitting the vanilla. Turn out onto a lightly floured surface, then roll out to ½ inch thick. Cut into rounds with the cutter, knead the trimmings together, re-roll, and cut more rounds. Omit the raw or white sugar. Arrange the rounds slightly apart on the prepared baking trays, then chill for about 15 minutes until firm. Bake as in the main recipe.

Omit the vanilla and raw or white sugar from the above ingredients, and add ½ cup shelled pistachio nuts, blanched, dried, and coarsely chopped

Makes about 14

This rich, grainy shortbread is *perfect* *with vanilla ice-cream.*
chocolate shortbread

Using a wooden spoon or electric mixer, beat the butter until creamy and light. Add the sugar and beat again until fluffy. Sift the flour with the cocoa and salt. Using a wooden spoon or your hands, work them into the mixture until it comes together. Knead gently for couple of seconds, then press the dough into the pan to make an even layer. Cover and chill for 15 minutes. Prick the dough well and score into 12 sections with a round-bladed knife. Bake the shortbread in a preheated oven at 350°F for 15 to 20 minutes—do not allow it to brown or it will taste bitter. Remove from the oven, sprinkle with superfine sugar or confectioners' sugar and cocoa, then cut into sections along the marked lines. Let cool before removing from the pan. Store in an airtight container and eat within 1 week, or freeze for up to 1 month.

¾ cup sweet butter, at room temperature

½ cup superfine or granulated sugar

1⅔ cups all-purpose flour

1½ oz. unsweetened cocoa

a good pinch of salt

extra sugar or confectioners' sugar, for sprinkling

one 9-inch round cake pan, greased

Makes 12 triangles

Only the **finest** *bitter chocolate is suitable for this recipe.*

bittersweet chocolate
butter cookies

2½ oz. unsweetened chocolate, coarsely chopped (preferably with at least 70 percent cocoa solids)

1½ tablespoons superfine or granulated sugar

1 cup sweet butter, chilled and diced

¾ cup light brown sugar

1⅔ cups all-purpose flour

½ teaspoon real vanilla extract

2 oz. white or unsweetened chocolate, melted, to decorate

several baking trays, well greased

Makes 30

Blend the chopped chocolate and sugar in a food processor until they form the texture of sand. Add the diced butter, brown sugar, flour, and vanilla, then process again until the dough just comes together.

Using your hands, form the dough into about 30 walnut-sized balls. Space well apart on the baking trays.

Bake the cookies in a preheated oven at 350°F for 10 to 15 minutes or until they are just firm to the touch and beginning to color around the edges.

Remove from the oven. They are very fragile at this stage, so leave them on the trays for 5 minutes before transferring to a wire rack to cool.

When completely cold, decorate by drizzling with the melted chocolate using either a fork or a greaseproof paper icing bag. Leave until firm, then store in an airtight container and eat within 4 days.

Undecorated cookies can be frozen for up to 1 month, but you may have to crisp them in a warm oven before decorating.

pecan lace cookies

Very gently melt the butter in a small pan, then let it cool while you prepare the other ingredients.

Blend the nuts, sugar, and flour in a food processor until the nuts are finely ground. With the machine still running, pour in the cream and butter through the food tube. Process until you have a soft dough.

Space heaped spoonfuls of the mixture well apart on the baking trays. Flatten them with a fork, then bake in a preheated oven at 350°F for 7 to 9 minutes or until they turn golden brown with slightly darker edges.

Let cool on the baking trays, then store in an airtight container and eat within 4 days. They do not freeze well.

These **delicate**, *elegant cookies are perfect to serve after-dinner with sorbets or little cups of strong, black, coffee.*

2 tablespoons sweet butter

1 cup chopped pecans or walnuts

½ cup superfine or granulated sugar

3 tablespoons all-purpose flour

2 tablespoons heavy cream

several baking trays, lined with non-stick waxed paper

Makes about 24

For **crunchy** *texture and intense almond taste, use freshly ground and whole nuts—toasted first—and real almond extract.*

almond crescents

1 stick sweet butter,
at room temperature

2–3 drops real almond extract
(not almond flavoring)

⅔ cup confectioners' sugar, sifted

a pinch of salt

⅔ cup all-purpose flour, sifted

1½ cups ground almonds

1½ oz. whole almonds,
lightly toasted then chopped

extra confectioners' sugar,
for dredging

several baking trays, greased

Makes about 22

Beat the butter and almond extract until light and creamy. Add the sifted sugar and, using a wooden spoon or electric mixer, mix slowly, then beat well until fluffy. Add the salt, flour, and ground almonds, then mix thoroughly with a wooden spoon. Mix in the chopped toasted almonds and, if necessary, knead the dough gently, just enough to bring it together.

Do not overwork the dough—it should be quite firm. In warm weather, you may need to wrap it and chill for 15 to 20 minutes to harden the dough to the proper consistency.

Using your hands, roll heaped teaspoonfuls of the dough into sausages about 3 inches long, curving each into a crescent. Space well apart on the prepared baking trays, then cook in a preheated oven at 325°F for 15 to 18 minutes or until firm. They should still be pale, with only the tops slightly browned. Let cool on the trays for about 2 minutes, then dredge with confectioners' sugar. Transfer the crescents to a wire rack to cool completely.

Store in an airtight container and eat within 1 week. This recipe does not freeze successfully.

For the best flavor, make the **strongest** *possible espresso coffee, then let it cool before using.*

espresso
walnut squares

1 cup all-purpose flour

a pinch of salt

¾ cup light brown sugar

7 tablespoons sweet butter,
chilled and diced

1 teaspoon baking powder

1 egg, beaten

3 tablespoons very strong
espresso coffee, cold

1 tablespoon milk

½ cup walnut pieces

one 8-inch square cake pan,
greased and base-lined

Makes 16 squares

Sift the flour, salt, and sugar into a mixing bowl. Add the cold chunks of butter and rub with your fingertips until the mixture resembles coarse crumbs. Set aside 4 tablespoons of the mixture. Add the baking powder to the rest and mix well. Combine the egg, coffee, and milk, then stir into the mixing bowl. When thoroughly combined, add three-quarters of the nuts. Spoon the mixture into the pan and level it.

Mix the remaining nuts with the reserved crumbs and sprinkle over the top.

Bake in a preheated oven at 350°F for 20 to 25 minutes until golden brown and firm to the touch.

Let cool for about 1 to 2 minutes, then run a palette knife around the edges of the pan to loosen it and carefully turn onto a wire rack.

Leave until completely cold before cutting into 16 squares. Store in an airtight container and eat within 4 days, or freeze for up to 1 month.

These cookies should always be made with the *freshest* nuts, best-quality chocolate, and good, *strong* espresso-style coffee.

mocha macaroons

Gently melt the chopped chocolate in a heatproof bowl set over a pan of barely simmering water. Remove from the heat and stir until smooth.

With a hand beater or electric mixer, beat the egg whites until they form stiff peaks. Gradually beat in the sugar, then fold in the almonds, coffee, and chocolate.

When well mixed, put heaped teaspoonfuls, spaced well apart, on the prepared baking trays. Spread into circles about 3 inches across and decorate with the almonds. Bake in a preheated oven at 300°F for about 25 minutes or until firm. Let cool, then peel off the paper or remove them from the greased tray. Transfer to a wire rack, and leave until completely cold.

Store in an airtight container and eat within 1 week. The macaroons do not freeze well.

3 oz. unsweetened chocolate, chopped

2 egg whites

1 cup superfine or granulated sugar

1½ cups ground almonds

1 tablespoon strong espresso coffee

sliced, split or slivered almonds, to decorate

several baking trays, well greased or lined with non-stick waxed paper

Makes 18

35

*Use **sugar-free** peanut butter in this recipe, or the cookies will be much too sweet.*

peanut butter and jelly
cookie sandwiches

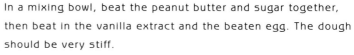

9½ oz. crunchy unsweetened peanut butter

¾ cup superfine or granulated sugar

2–3 drops real vanilla extract

1 large egg, beaten

about 4 tablespoons raspberry jam or redcurrant jelly, for the filling

several baking trays, well greased

Makes about 12 sandwiches

In a mixing bowl, beat the peanut butter and sugar together, then beat in the vanilla extract and the beaten egg. The dough should be very stiff.

Divide the dough into 24 pieces and roll them into balls with your hands. Space the pieces well apart on the baking trays, then flatten with a fork.

Bake in a preheated oven at 350°F for about 12 to 15 minutes or until golden brown. Leave on the trays for a few minutes to firm up, then transfer to a wire rack until completely cold.

Sandwich pairs of cookies together with a little jam or jelly. Store in an airtight container and eat within 1 week.

The cookies can be frozen for up to 1 month, but they must be frozen without the jam or jelly filling.

Note: *this recipe is suitable for people on gluten-free diets, and for serving during Passover.*

An **elegant** *combination of white nuts, white chocolate.*

white chocolate
macadamia nut crumbles

1⅓ cups all-purpose flour

a pinch of salt

½ teaspoon baking powder

1 stick plus 2½ tablespoons sweet butter, at room temperature

½ cup superfine or granulated sugar

1 egg, lightly beaten

½ teaspoon real vanilla extract

5½ oz. good-quality white chocolate, coarsely chopped

3 oz. unsalted macadamia nuts, coarsely chopped

several baking trays, lightly greased

Makes about 24

Sift the flour, salt, and baking powder into a bowl.

In another bowl, cream the butter and sugar until fluffy using a wooden spoon or electric mixer.

Beat in the egg and, when thoroughly mixed, stir in the flour mixture with a large metal spoon. When no streaks are visible, stir in the vanilla, chocolate, and nuts.

Put tablespoons of the mixture, spaced well apart, on the prepared baking trays. Bake in a preheated oven at 350°F for 10 to 12 minutes until firm but not colored. Leave the cookies to cool on the trays for a minute, then transfer to a wire rack to cool completely.

Store in an airtight container and eat within 5 days. These cookies do not freeze well.

Walnuts make wonderful cookies, but **pecans** *or* **hazelnuts** *will also work well in this recipe.*

walnut cookies

½ cup walnut pieces, chopped

7 tablespoons sweet butter, at room temperature

3½ tablespoons superfine or granulated sugar

3 tablespoons raw or white sugar

1 large egg, beaten

½ teaspoon real vanilla extract

1⅔ cups self-rising flour

several baking trays, greased

Makes 24

Walnuts can sometimes be very bitter, and can also turn rancid very quickly when exposed to air, so taste one first before using them in this recipe.

Using a wooden spoon or electric mixer, beat the butter until soft and creamy. Gradually beat in the sugars and continue beating for another 2 minutes.

Beat in the egg a little at a time, then stir in the vanilla, flour, and chopped nuts. Work the mixture with your hands until it comes together into a firm dough. Again using your hands, roll the dough into 24 walnut-sized balls.

Space them well apart on the baking trays, then flatten with a fork. Bake in a preheated oven at 350°F for about 10 minutes or until golden and firm.

Leave on the trays for a couple of minutes to firm up, then transfer to a wire rack to cool completely.

Store in an airtight container and eat within 1 week, or freeze for up to 1 month.

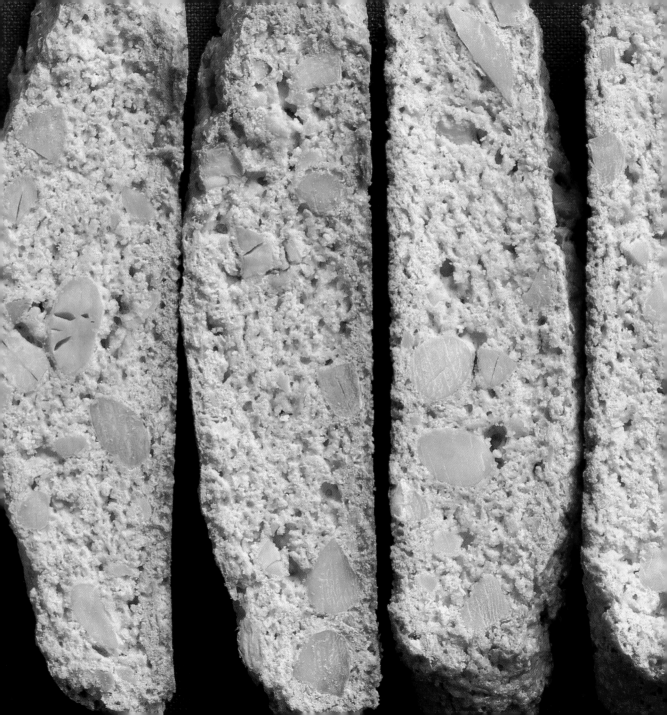

almond biscotti

¾ cup blanched almonds

1⅔ cups all-purpose flour

½ cup plus 1 tablespoon
vanilla sugar, if available,
sugar, or superfine sugar

¾ teaspoon baking powder

2 large eggs, plus 1 yolk

½ teaspoon real almond
extract or vanilla extract

a baking tray, greased

Makes about 20

Twice-baked biscotti from Tuscany—served after dinner with fresh fruit and a glass of sweet Vin Santo wine for dipping and sipping.

Toast the almonds on a heatproof dish in a preheated oven at 350°F for 10 to 12 minutes until lightly browned. Cool, then coarsely chop ½ cup of the nuts and set aside.

Put the remainder in a food processor or blender and grind to a fine powder.

Mix the ground almonds in a mixing bowl with the flour, sugar, and baking powder. Make a well in the center. Beat the eggs with the yolk and the almond or vanilla extract and pour into the well. Gradually work the flour mixture into the eggs, then add the chopped almonds. Knead very well to bring the dough together—do not add any extra liquid.

Divide the dough in half and shape each piece into a flat log about 10 x 2½ x ¾ inch. Place the logs well apart on the baking tray. Bake at 350°F for about 25 minutes until golden and firm to the touch.

Remove from the oven and let cool for about 5 minutes. Reduce the oven temperature to 325°F.

Transfer the logs to a cutting board then, using a serrated knife, gently and carefully cut them diagonally into slices about ¾ inch thick. Arrange the slices, cut side up, on the baking tray and bake for a further 10 to 12 minutes at 325°F until golden and crisp.

Cool on a wire rack, then store in an airtight container and eat within 2 weeks.

*Traditional biscotti, flavored with fennel seeds, are served as a digestif. These are **modern** variations.*

cinnamon and raisin
biscotti

Put the almonds on a heatproof dish and toast in the oven for 10 to 12 minutes until lightly browned. Cool and leave whole. Beat the egg, sugar, and vanilla in a bowl, by hand or with an electric mixer, until very thick and pale (ribbons of mixture should trail from the beater as you lift it out of the bowl). Sift the flour, baking powder, salt, and cinnamon onto a piece of waxed paper, then sift again into the mixing bowl. Stir until thoroughly combined with the egg mixture, then stir in the raisins and almonds. Turn out the mixture onto the prepared tray and shape it into a flat log about 10 x 2½ x ¾ inch. Bake the log in a preheated oven at 350°F for about 20 to 25 minutes or until golden brown. Let cool for about 5 minutes, or until firm, then transfer to a cutting board. With a serrated bread knife, cut the log on the diagonal into slices about ½ inch thick. Arrange on the tray, and bake again for 10 to 15 minutes or until golden. Allow to rest for 5 minutes, then transfer to a wire rack to cool completely. Store in an airtight container and eat within 2 weeks.

Variation:
Chocolate Biscotti
Omit the raisins and cinnamon and add 2 oz. unsweetened chocolate chunks with the nuts. Proceed as in the main recipe.

2 oz. whole blanched almonds

1 large egg

½ cup superfine or granulated sugar

1 teaspoon real vanilla extract

¾ cup all-purpose flour

½ teaspoon baking powder

a pinch of salt

¾ teaspoon ground cinnamon

2 oz. raisins

a baking tray, well greased

Makes about 20

French tuiles are **perfect** *with ice-cream or fruit salads.*
orange tuiles

Put the egg whites in a spotlessly clean, grease-free, non-plastic bowl. Using a hand or electric beater, beat slowly at first, then increase the speed until the egg whites form stiff peaks. Gradually beat in the sugar, then the cooled melted butter and finally the sifted flour. If you use an electric mixer, keep it on low speed.

Gently stir in the grated orange rind and the liqueur, if using. Spoon 1 teaspoon of the mixture onto a prepared baking tray and spread it into a thin disc about 4 inches across. Bake in a preheated oven at 350°F for about 5 minutes or until it turns a very pale gold.

Remove from the oven and, using a palette knife, immediately loosen it from the sheet and drape over a rolling pin. It will harden very rapidly into a U-shape. Remove and set aside. Once you have the knack, bake the tuiles 2 at a time. Store in an airtight container, and eat within 2 days—humidity or damp makes them uncurl, so store with care. These cookies are not suitable for freezing.

2 egg whites, at room temperature

**⅔ cup superfine
or granulated sugar**

**4½ tablespoons sweet butter,
melted and cooled**

½ cup all-purpose flour, sifted

grated rind of 1 unwaxed orange

**1 teaspoon orange liqueur
(optional)**

several baking trays, greased

Makes about 18

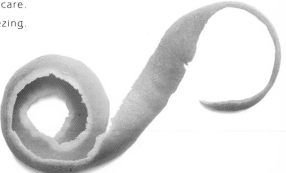

Just a hint of cinnamon makes these delicate, lacy cookies an excellent match for ice-cream, sorbets, or mousses.

danish cookies

1½ sticks sweet butter

2 cups rolled oats

1 cup plus 2 tablespoons
superfine or granulated sugar

2 eggs, beaten

1 tablespoon all-purpose flour

2 teaspoons baking powder

1 teaspoon ground cinnamon

several baking trays,
well greased or lined with
non-stick waxed paper

Makes about 24

Melt the butter gently in a medium saucepan. Remove from the heat and stir in the rolled oats. When thoroughly combined, add the remaining ingredients and mix well.

These cookies are best baked in batches of three. (Cook the batches on one baking tray while the other is cooling down). Space 3 mounds—each about 1 heaped teaspoonful of the mixture—well apart on a baking tray.

Bake in a preheated oven at 350°F for about 5 to 7 minutes or until golden brown.

Using a spatula, immediately lift the baked cookies off the sheet and let cool upside down on a wire rack. Repeat the process until all the mixture is used.

These cookies quickly lose their crispness in damp or humid conditions, so store carefully in an airtight container and eat within 4 days. They do not freeze well.

irish whiskey fingers

1 unwaxed lemon

1 cup golden raisins

½ tablespoons whiskey

1 stick plus 1 tablespoon sweet
butter, at room temperature

⅔ cup superfine
or granulated sugar

2 large eggs, separated

¾ cup self-rising flour

1–2 tablespoons
raw or white sugar

one 7-inch square cake pan,
greased and base-lined

Cuts into 10 fingers

Soak the fruit in whiskey the night before baking— Irish gives the **best flavor,** *but Scotch is very good too.*

Using a vegetable peeler, pare off the rind of the lemon and put it into a small bowl. Add the golden raisins, then pour over the whiskey. Cover tightly and leave overnight.

With a wooden spoon or electric mixer, beat the butter until creamy. Beat in the sugar and continue beating until the mixture is very light and fluffy.

Beat in the egg yolks one at a time. Remove the lemon rind, then add the golden raisins and whiskey to the cake mixture, carefully folding them in with a metal spoon.

In another bowl, whisk the egg whites until they form stiff peaks, then fold them into the mixture in 3 batches alternately with batches of the flour.

Spoon into the prepared pan and smooth the surface. Sprinkle with the raw or white sugar, then bake in a preheated oven at 350°F for about 25 minutes, or until just firm to the touch. Remove from the oven, let rest in the pan for about 5 minutes, then carefully unmold the cake onto a wire rack. Leave until completely cold, then cut into fingers.

Store in an airtight container and eat within 1 week, or freeze for up to 1 month.

For *authentic* taste, make these *vanilla-scented French cookies with best-quality sweet butter.*

sablés

Mix the flour, salt, confectioners' sugar, and diced butter in a food processor until the mixture resembles fine sand. Add the egg yolks and vanilla, and process again until the mixture comes together as a firm dough. Turn it out of the processor, cover in plastic wrap, and chill for 15 minutes. On a lightly floured work surface, roll out the chilled dough to about ¼ inch thick, then cut out rounds with the fluted cutter. Space them a little apart on the baking trays. Knead the trimmings together, roll again, cut more rounds, and arrange them on the trays. Brush the rounds very lightly with beaten egg, then chill for 15 minutes. Brush again with the egg glaze, prick all over with a fork, then mark with the prongs to make a neat pattern. Bake the cookies in a preheated oven at 350°F for about 12 to 15 minutes or until golden brown. Remove from the oven, leave on the baking trays for a few seconds to firm up, then carefully transfer to a wire rack. Let cool completely, then store in an airtight container, and eat within 1 week, or freeze for up to 1 month.

1⅓ cups all-purpose flour

a pinch of salt

¾ cup confectioners' sugar

1 cup plus 1 tablespoon sweet butter, chilled and diced

3 egg yolks

½ teaspoon real vanilla extract

1 egg, beaten, to glaze

one 3½-inch fluted cookie cutter

several baking trays, greased

Makes about 10

FINGERS **AND** **BARS**

If using whole cardamoms, remove the pods and crush the black seeds with a mortar and pestle.

sour cream

cardamom squares

1⅔ cups self-rising flour

½ teaspoon baking soda

a pinch of salt

¼ teaspoon ground cardamom

1½ sticks sweet butter, at room temperature

1¼ cups superfine or granulated sugar

3 large eggs

⅔ cup sour cream

confectioners' sugar, for dusting

one 8-inch square cake pan, greased and base-lined

Makes 9

Sift the flour with the baking soda, salt, and ground cardamom, then set aside.

With a wooden spoon or electric mixer, cream the butter. Gradually beat in the sugar and continue beating until the mixture is very light and fluffy.

Add the eggs one at a time, beating well after each addition. With a large metal spoon, fold in the flour mixture in 3 batches, alternating with the sour cream.

Spoon the mixture into the prepared cake pan and smooth the surface. Bake in a preheated oven at 350°F for 45 minutes or until golden brown and firm to the touch. Loosen the edges with a round-bladed knife, then turn onto a wire rack. When completely cold, cut into 9 squares, and dust with confectioners' sugar. Store in an airtight container and eat within 1 week, or freeze for up to 1 month.

mincemeat crumble

Sift the flour, salt, and cinnamon into a mixing bowl. Rub in the diced butter with your fingertips until the mixture resembles fine crumbs. Stir in the sugar, diced apple, dried fruit, and peel. Mix the egg and the milk, and stir them into the mixture to make a soft dough.
Spread the dough evenly in the prepared pan and sprinkle with the raw or white sugar.
Bake in a preheated oven at 400°F for about 20 minutes or until firm and golden. Remove from the oven, let cool for 1 minute, then cut into 9 squares.
Let cool completely, then store in an airtight container, eat within 4 days, or freeze for up to 1 month.

Variation:

Dried Fruit, Pineapple, and Apricot Crumble
Omit the apple and substitute 1 cup of one of the luxury dried fruit mixtures, containing pineapple and apricot, that are often available around holiday time.

Crisp, *tart* apples are best for this quick and *easy* crumble.

1½ cups self-rising flour

a pinch of salt

½ teaspoon ground cinnamon

6½ tablespoons sweet butter, chilled and diced

3½ tablespoons raw or white sugar

1 medium apple, peeled, cored, and diced

¾ cup mixed dried fruit and peel

1 large egg

4 tablespoons milk

1–2 tablespoons raw or white sugar, for sprinkling

one 8-inch square cake pan, greased

Makes 9

pecan spice bars

7 tablespoons sweet butter, at room temperature

3 tablespoons golden syrup* or corn syrup

1 large egg

1¼ cups self-rising flour

a pinch of salt

¼ teaspoon grated nutmeg

½ teaspoon ground cinnamon

¼ teaspoon ground ginger

1 cup coarsely ground pecans

1½ tablespoons milk

Spicy Pecan Topping:

2 tablespoons flour

2 tablespoons light brown sugar

¼ teaspoon grated nutmeg

¼ teaspoon grated ginger

2½ tablespoons sweet butter, diced

1 oz. pecan halves

one 8-inch square cake pan, greased and lined

Makes 15

*Available in larger supermarkets.

Using a wooden spoon or electric mixer, cream the butter until light and fluffy. Beat in the golden syrup or corn syrup, then gradually beat in the egg.

Sift the flour with the salt and spices, then stir into the mixture together with the ground pecans and milk. When all the base ingredients are thoroughly combined, spoon the mixture into the prepared pan and smooth the surface.

To make the topping, first mix the flour with the sugar and spices. Work in the butter with your fingers to make small clumps of dough. Stir in the pecans.

Sprinkle the clumps over the base mixture in the pan, then bake in a preheated oven at 350°F for about 25 to 30 minutes until firm to the touch.

Remove the cake in its paper lining from the pan. Let cool, then slice into 15 pieces. Store in an airtight container and eat within 1 week, or freeze up to 1 month.

An excellent combination of moist sponge base and crunchy topping of nuts and spices.

*Use only genuine maple syrup for a more **intense** flavor.*

New England maple syrup pecan bars

Heat the butter, sugar, and syrup gently in a medium-sized saucepan, stirring occasionally, until dissolved. Remove from the heat, stir in the oats and nuts, and mix well. Spread evenly in the prepared pan, pressing down lightly. Using a sharp knife, score the mixture into 10 rectangles. Bake in a preheated oven at 300°F for about 25 to 30 minutes or until golden.

Remove from the oven, and cut along the scored lines. Do not remove the bars from the pan until they are completely cold. Store in an airtight container and eat within 1 week, or freeze for up to 1 month.

Variations:

Dried Fruit, Chocolate, Spice, or Nut Bars

Omit the pecans and maple syrup, and use 1 tablespoon golden syrup* or corn syrup instead. Instead of the nuts, add one of the following: 1 oz. raisins, 1 oz. chocolate pieces, 1 teaspoon ground ginger, 1½ oz. each of chopped dates and walnut pieces, 1½ oz. chopped almonds and a few drops almond extract, or 1½ oz. chopped mixed nuts together with 1½ oz. soft dried apricots.

Available in larger supermarkets and gourmet shops.

1¼ sticks sweet butter

⅔ cup light brown sugar

1 tablespoon maple syrup

2½ cups rolled oats

½ cup pecans, coarsely chopped

one 7-inch square cake pan, well-greased

Makes 10

tangy lemon bars

¾ cup all-purpose flour

a pinch of salt

⅓ cup confectioners' sugar

¾ stick sweet butter, chilled

3 drops real vanilla extract

Lemon Topping:

2 eggs

⅞ cup sugar

the grated rind and juice
of 1 large unwaxed lemon

1 tablespoon all-purpose flour

½ teaspoon baking soda

confectioners' sugar, for dusting

one 8-inch square cake pan,
well greased

Makes 12

Put the flour, salt, and confectioners' sugar into a food processor and combine well. Dice the butter and add to the processor with the vanilla. Process until the mixture comes together to make a firm dough.

Press the dough into the base of the prepared pan to make an even layer. Prick well with a fork and, if the weather is very warm, chill for 15 minutes.

Bake in a preheated oven at 350°F for about 12 to 15 minutes until firm and slightly golden but not browned. Let cool in the pan while making the topping.

Using an electric beater or mixer, beat the eggs in a bowl until frothy. Gradually beat in the sugar and continue until the mixture is thick and foamy. Beat in the lemon rind and juice, then the flour and baking soda. Pour the mixture over the base and bake for 20 to 25 minutes until golden brown.

Let cool in the pan, then divide into 12 rectangles.

Store in an airtight container and eat within 4 days. This recipe does not freeze well.

*A crisp, buttery base with a sticky topping and a **sharp** citrus tang.*